Preface

To the reader

Knowing is half the fight and Cooking is the other was written with you in mind every step of the way. I am the kind of man who likes to get straight to the point and I hope that at the end of this book I have achieved that. This book will show you the small things that you can do to positively affect your health. I will give you facts, suggestions, and steps that you can start doing as soon as possible to change your overall health. Yes, this book is brief; but healthy living isn't complicated. I hope that after you read this book cover to cover you truly find information and tips to take away. This book is meant to be digested slowly, so take your time and master a couple steps before moving to the next. With that being said, thank you for your interest and remember "Yesterday is out of your reach, but tomorrow can be in your hands", SuperChef.

The Chef Behind the Book

I am Darnell "SuperChef" Ferguson, a young and enthusiastic chef who was born in Philadelphia and raised in the great city of Columbus, Ohio. Even though I consider myself an "Ohio Boy", the great city of Louisville, Kentucky has helped to mold me into the man I am today. The path that I took to write this book was a long and enlightening one. I first started off by cooking morning breakfast as a child with my cousins on the weekends and never knew what kind of journey would lie ahead for me. I signed up for Culinary Arts in vocational school during my junior year in high school thinking that maybe I would like it- and if I didn't; I would at least eat well (LOL). But things changed; from being okay at cooking to my teacher having me think (without saying it) that I could be something special at it. She motivated me through her actions by staying on my back and never letting me second guess my culinary skills.

Shortly after attending vocational school, I also started to do better in high school and before I knew it, I was for sure that cooking was what I was going to do to help change my life in a positive way. I grew up in an environment in which I was accustomed to seeing my friends get killed and seeing a lot of people around me sell drugs and not finish school. But having a caring mother who supported me and having the WILL to

WANT more out of life, set me up for an amazing future. Since then, I have graduated from one of the top culinary institutes in the nation, Sullivan University, with my degree in culinary arts and [my master's in thinking ahead of the crowd].

I've had the honor of being a chef at the 2008 Summer Olympics in China at the USA House. I have been blessed with the opportunity to cook for the former President of the United States, George Bush Senior, and I have cooked for various governors and mayors. I have also cooked at some of the top restaurants and country clubs in Louisville, Kentucky. On top of all the blessings I have already stated, I also have been on the Rachel Ray Show, Food Network, Cooking Channel, HLN and spent time with my culinary inspiration Emeril Lagasse. As you can see, my passion is geared toward being a personal chef and enlightening people on how to cook for themselves.

I have always felt that when you love something, it becomes a part of you and that's what cooking did- I didn't just want to know how to cook; I wanted to understand the food. I wanted to know not only how certain foods could taste if I cooked them a certain way but also how would those foods would affect my health. Since I am still young, whenever I don't know something I ask why. The answers given by most chefs are long and confusing. So, once I figured out my problems on my own; I learned how to translate it to people in a normal dialogue and that's where I dreamt up *Knowing is Half the Fight, and Cooking is the Other*. When there is no enemy within, the enemy on the outside can do you no harm. I am a true believer that you must get yourself together before you can get any external wants accomplished. There comes a time in everyone's life where you must focus on you and your wellbeing. I have seen Americans try to live healthier lives but I've also seen them throw a lot of nonsense into their brains. So, I've tried to simplify everything for you and hear it is...

The 1st part of living a healthier lifestyle is mental health. Healing will always take part inside 1st and then outward. You must combat all the negative thoughts that you have in your head. Only tell yourself the things that make you into who you truly know you are deep down inside. You should think the things into existence that you want before they happen. The biggest obstacle in whatever you will be trying to accomplish will be yourself. You must put time and effort into the things that make up the person you are; once you do that, the world can't stop you! One of the most powerful statements I have ever heard was when I was listening to a motivational speech by Les Brown and he said, "Life is 1% what happens to you and 99% what you do with it"! It's time we start affecting the world and stop being an effect of it. This book is meant to add value to your life, but the most important value comes from what you already have inside you. The heart and spirit that God gave you that you must start to unlock.

> *Mental food- You must stir up the gifts of God, just like sugar in lemonade, it may be there but it must be set in motion- unknown*

Moderation is Key to Healthy Eating

TIPS:

Portion control is crucial

Portion control is the central reason why we as Americans are gaining so much weight. You should be aware of what a true portion size looks like and believe me: your normal portion size and the recommended portion size are on two different levels. It's kind of like putting unleaded gas in a premium car, you have the right intent but just the wrong knowledge. For instance did

you know one portion of cereal is one cup.

We grow up our entire lives pouring cereal

until the bowl was full, never knowing that

we should had less cereal and maybe some

fresh fruit with it. A good tip you should try

is using smaller plates when you eat that

way it looks like you're eating more than

you are. A little thing like serving dinner on

8 inch plates instead of 10 inch can have a

huge effect of how much you eat. Eating is

11

just as much mental as physical, how much you see on your plate also determines if you feel you have had enough to eat. In a later section, we will go through in details what some recommend serving sizes are.

Another great tip is to learn to eyeball what a correct amount of protein, starch, or veggies should look like; for instance, your amount of rice should be about the size of a baseball.

mental food- focus on the opportunity not the obligation- E.T.

Try and eat at least the lowest number of servings from each food group

When eating healthy, you don't have to make sure you have the maximum amount of recommend servings in the beginning- just try and get the minimum amount on average for the week in the beginning of this change from the old thought pattern to the new ones. Eating should be joyful; it shouldn't feel like you are studying for a test-LOL. This is a process and I truly believe you should start at the bottom and work your way up.

mental food - There is no elevator to success; you have to take the stairs.

Ordering pizza is okay every once in a while

Ordering pizza or eating out with the family is not bad when done in **moderation;** though it becomes harmful when you are constantly ordering out. Ordering pizza should be used just on special occasion; for example, if your child has done well in a game or if you have had a long week at work and truly are just exhausted. I remember that when I was growing up, going out to eat was a lot fun because it wasn't a part of our normal lives. Now, just as people say TV is raising our kids, so are restaurants and fast food.

* *Mental food- To much of a good thing can destroy you*

*Planning is very important when living a healthy lifestyle

Planning is key in making eating healthy easier. You don't jump into a car and just start driving, do you? (especially with these high gas prices) No! You know where you're going and how to get there. Why not have the same mindset when it pertains to cooking? Planning what you are going to have for the week on Sunday gives you the chance to make a trip to the supermarket to get everything you will need. This way, when it comes time to cook, you're not stressing out about missing an ingredient. With places like Kroger and Walmart allowing you to place your grocery order online, planning ahead is a must and

not to mention they put the groceries in the

car for you! How much easier can this get

for us?? Planning also allows you to make

substitutions; for instance, if you see that

you're eating a lot of meat one week you

can rotate in pasta and other dishes to take

the meat's place.

Mental food- If you fail to plan then you plan to fail, a great quote from the one and only, Rev Run

When you cook it's okay to make too much- that way you can freeze it and make it a meal later in the week

You not only want to cook healthy- you also want to cook smart. Why not try to eliminate some of your time in the kitchen while eating more home cooked meals? Once during the week, you should purposely cook too much food so that you can freeze it and thaw it out a couple days later.

Mental food- Sometimes it's okay to kill two birds with one stone.

Learning your serving sizes

If you are wondering what an actual serving size is for each food group, I've put together a few samples below to guide you. Remember, everything depends on your age, sex, and level of physical activity. Portion sizes are also based on the daily nutrition recommendations.

Grains: Recommended 6 ounces

An ounce is equivalent to 1\2 cup cooked rice, 1 cup of cereal, or one slice of bread.

Fruits & Veggie: Recommended 2-3 cups

A cup is equivalent to 1 cup of veggies, 1 cup of 100 percent vegetable juice or fruit, 2 cups of greens, one apple, orange, or banana, or 1\2 cup of chopped or canned fruit.

Milk& Dairy: Recommended 3 cups (should choose low-fat)

A cup is equivalent to 1 1\2 ounce of natural cheese, 2 ounces processed cheese, or 1 cup of milk or yogurt.

Meat (also includes beans, fish, eggs, nuts and seeds): Recommended 2-3 servings

This is the one food group from which we don't need to worry about getting enough- the problem is eating too much. You should try if possible to make each serving of meat around 6 ounces. One ounce is equivalent to one egg, 1\2 cup

cooked dry beans, 1\3 cup nuts, or two

tablespoons of peanut butter.

Mental food- to do better, you have to know

better.

Having the right measuring utensils on

hand makes life easier

Measuring cups, measuring spoons,

and an inexpensive scale should be staples

in your kitchen. You don't just need these

items to cook, but you also need them to put the correct amount of food on your plate. The only way to know that you are eating the right amount of food is to measure it; at least until you get an eye for portion sizes.

Mental food- If the only tool you have is a hammer you tend to see every problem as a nail- Abraham Maslow

Whenever you're feeling hungry, try eating fruit or something filling yet healthy first!

Try this out for a change: put out a small fruit dish for everyone to snack on before dinner. It's a healthy way to prepare your stomach for what's next- LOL. It will help you tone down your hunger so that you're not trying to go back for seconds.

Most veggies are high in fiber and will start filling you up without you even knowing.

Mental food- Most fights are won by how you prepare for them!

Know the difference between hunger and cravings-

A lot of people eat when they are hungry which is natural, but most of us also eat when we experience cravings (that would be that fourth meal you had

yesterday from Taco Bell). Craving is when

you *desire* something, and hunger is when

you *need* food. The problem with the two is

that when people are craving certain things,

they usually eat as if they are hungry which

turns that craving into another meal.

Cravings are usually mental or sensual

(meaning you smelled something or saw

something you liked). Your body may not

need food when you experiencing a craving,

but we still tend to eat- and that's when

those calories add up. Try to incorporate

your cravings into one of your meals

throughout the day.

Mental food- Some people like to have their

cake, and eat it too

Eat slow and only until you're satisfied

Have you ever wondered why the

person next to you may be the same size as

you and orders the same thing as you, but

doesn't even finish their plate before you're

finished eating? The reason they don't clean

their plate may help you realize that you

are over eating while your dinning partner

is eating slower. Eating slower gives you a

chance to truly savor the taste of what

you're eating and gives your brain enough

time to tell your body that it's full. You may

have been able to stop eating before you

were done with your plate, but people eat

so fast that they never give their bodies and minds a chance to work together. Look on the flip side- if you stuff your face, you're going to eat everything on your plate for the most part, and when you're done, you'll be full and slower, while the person who ate just enough is still satisfied and alert.

mental food- You don't get what you want out of life, you get what you must have- E.T

Why Soft Drinks Suck

This section is all about why you

should reduce your consumption of soft

drinks. I want to give you a little insight on

how soft drinks affect your body. If people

knew what they did to your overall health, I

know we wouldn't continue consuming

soooo much! Please bear with me through

this section because it may seem as if you are in health class during your sophomore year in high school, but sometimes the easiest way to gain knowledge is to not sugar coat it- no pun intended (lol).

* Most soft drinks (12 ounces) contain around 10 teaspoons of sugar.

* When you drink a lot of soda, you must realize that these drinks are packed with simple syrups that have almost no positive affect on your health- in fact, these syrups

raise your insulin levels. Once your insulin level rises too high, it can lead to the depression of your immune system and weakening your ability to fight off disease.

* Studies have shown that one or more soft drinks a day, no matter if regular or diet, can lead to a 30 percent greater chance of weight gain around the belly.

* Much weight gain can come from excess sugar being stored as fat, which will also

increase your chances of experiencing heart

disease and cancer.

* Diet sodas are not good for you either:

they contain artificial sweeteners, such as

Aspartame and Saccharin, which are not

good for brain function. Aspartame

(NutraSweet) is a chemical found in almost

everything to replace sugar; it stimulates

the brain to think that food is sweet which

can in the end make you crave sweets. I

don't know about you but I don't want

anyone playing games with my brain, it's

just tooooooo important!

Why Aspartame is not good:

* When digested, it breaks down into three

chemical: aspartic acid, phenylalanine, and

methanol. I know those are really big

words, but it's the effects that it has on

your health are even bigger.

*Aspartic acid is a toxin that causes serious

chronic neurological disorders (and may be

a causal element in seizures).

* Phenylalanine decreases your serotonin levels, which can lead to emotional disorders, poor sleep, and depression.

* The carbonation in soft drinks depletes your calcium blood levels due to the chemical phosphoric acid found in all drinks with carbonation. Calcium is a key component in the makeup of our bones. **Drinking carbonated water, soft drinks, and anything else with carbonation raises your risk of osteoporosis.**

* If you consume fruit drinks, try diluting them a little bit with water to cut back the amount of sugar. Or, try drinking tea which has a positive effect on your health.

Remember: this book is not telling you what you have to do every day, but more of what you should do on average-nobody's perfect.

* *Mental food- Sometimes our greatest Joy is our deadliest attraction.*

Cook versatile

Cooking or eating versatile meals gives you variety which is important when eating healthy. It's so easy to get bored with the same food and same dishes. Don't just fry chicken: you should grill it, braise it, sauté it or put it in soups. Start doing themed nights by having, Chinese one night and then Italian the next. Keep it interesting. Americans have the reputation of not trying new things but that will change once we stop eating the same thing day in and day out. That's the biggest perk about eating healthy: you get to try new things!

Mental food- The greatest joy in life is found in exploring things you do not know.

Keep fresh produce in the fridge for a late-night snack

Yeah, we all know it's not healthy to eat late at night but if you think you're hungry, you will eat. Help yourself to make smarter decisions at night. Fresh fruit or veggies with dip are a great late night snack-they're healthy and delicious; and remember, you shouldn't have the same fruit every night. Take a trip to your local farmer's market with the kids and see what's new and in season. Guacamole and blue corn chips are my favorite late night snack.

Mental food- if you give up at the 1st sign of adversity, you're not ready to succeed.

Buy Produce that's in season

When you do buy produce, for the most part try to stay with what's in season because it usually has the most nutrients and the most flavor. What makes in-season even better is that it is usually the least expensive. If possible, I always tell people to go to a farmers' market because the produce there is picked closer to its peak of ripeness-unlike at Wal-Mart where whenever you buy bananas they are green and too firm. I hate that I must wait 2 days

before I can even eat them.

Mental food- the harvest is plentiful, but the

workers are few- Matthew 9:37

Try to eat whole grains when possible

Whenever there is an option to choose

whole grains, don't miss out. Yes, there is a

difference between wheat and whole grain

wheat: whole grain wheat contains the

entire wheat kernel (bran, germ,

endosperm), where-as wheat contains

refined grains that have been milled and

the germ and bran had been removed. Just

think about it like this: if you were at a car

dealership and they had two cars for the

same price, but one was fully loaded, which

one would you choose? You have to think

the same way with your health. Also, when

the bran and germ are removed, other

things are removed too, such as dietary

fiber, iron, and B Vitamins. Whole grains

also digest evenly and give you more energy

that lasts longer.

*Mental food- Success is making all the small

choices correctly.*

Slow down on prepared foods (heat and eat)

What I mean by slowdown is to

eventually quit. Prepared foods have to be

one of the leading causes of obesity and

high blood pressure. There are so many

chemicals used to preserve the food that

it's almost harmful for you to eat those foods; in fact, 99.9 percent of all prepared foods are processed. When I say processed, I'm talking about anything that has been added to the food that is not natural; for example, chemicals, coloring, or any additives. Microwave food is so cheap compared to making fresh meals and the reason is because you're getting what you've paid for: nothing.

Mental food- When you pay too much, you lose a little money- that's all. When you pay too little, you sometimes lose everything- John Ruskin

Know what you're eating

Sounds stupid, right? Wrong: you wouldn't believe how many people come into my restaurant, SuperChefs and ask for some of the "yellow sauce." What is yellow sauce (LoL)? It has a proper name, and I would think that most people would want to know what it actually is. It's called

"HONEY MUSTARD" and for someone who is allergic to honey, or any ingredient that's in mustard. I would think it's very important that they know what they're about to eat. The only way to truly eat healthy is to know what it is that you're eating. If you do eat out, be sure to ask a lot of questions about what foods you are ordering.

Mental food- knowing is half the fight, cooking is the other- no pun intended.

Reduce your intake of fast food

One of the main reasons why fast food is bad is because it has very little healthy options that are appealing and because people don't pick smart options. Do you see how this is a two-way street? They are serving bad food, but on the other hand YOUR BUYING IT. There is no one holding a gun to your head forcing you to order that Monster Thick Burger which has 1,420 calories in it. There is a way to get a healthier burger with the same great taste.

Many people are under the impression that ordering off the dollar menu is cheaper-but no, they're wrong. Once you price out how much ground beef costs and then break it down into correct portion sizes, it is cheaper and healthier to make your own burger at home. But we have become a people of convenience, not quality. We were created for community but fast food has taken away one of the most important places in the world.... The dinner table!

Mental Food- Time is already killing us, don't let the food we eat help it out!

No saturated fats or Trans fats

This is one of those points people need to really understand. At this point, I don't think there is one other thing that America can change to positively affect their health other than to stop the consumption of saturated fats and trans fats. Start using mono-saturated fats such as olive oil. Saturated fats (butter, lard, and margarine) have more negative effects than positive?

Olive oil has numerous positive effects

compared to negative; for example, it can:

* Help your cardio- it increases your good

HDL cholesterol and lowers your bad LDL

cholesterol. It also reduces your

triglycerides (forms of fat in the blood).

* Help keep your blood pressure down and

reduce your risk of cancer. Olive oil comes

from a plant (as if we all didn't already

know) and inside the plant is an antioxidant

called polyphenols which should get all the

credit.

Real life result: I was reading about a study

that was done on eight overweight men- to

keep it short and sweet, I'll get right to the

point. They all ate the same amount of food

for four weeks, but four of them ate only

mono-saturated fats while the other four

mainly consumed saturated fats.

Remember- they ate the same amount of

food and didn't increase physical activity

and at the end of the four weeks, the four who ate only mono-saturated fats were lighter and had lower body fat indexes. It's true: the proof is in the pudding.

Mental food- it's important to weigh your options before you make a decision.

Don't choose convenience over quality

Some people may call it a problem, but it's more of an epidemic. People are settling for fast food because it's convenient not because it's what they really want. You

have to be disciplined (which is not

punishment but training) when it comes to

eating healthier and you can take one of

your first steps here. I can recall plenty of

times when I pulled up to that drive- thru

speaker and couldn't find anything that I

really wanted to order but as I was too lazy

to cook at home, I'd settle for a burger with

luke-warm fries. We as people must truly

start to treat our bodies as temples: it's the

only one we have. I bet that if you had a really expensive car, you wouldn't put cheap gas in it, would you? Probably not. So, don't do the same with your most important car (your body).

* Mental food- So whether you eat or drink or whatever you do, do it all for the glory of God- 1 Corinthians 10:31

All food, if eaten in *moderation,* can be part of a healthy life

I think this will be everyone's favorite topic: yes, it's true that all food can be a part of a healthy diet. The key to this truth is the word moderation which means "the avoidance of excess" or not over excessively doing. I don't think that there is anything wrong with eating fried foods every once in a while. I feel the main reason why people are not eating in moderation is because they have hit a wall at home when it comes to cooking and they do what they know.

Mental food- They stopped searching, so they haven't found, they stopped wanting, so they never have.

Food is one of the top things that brings people pleasure

I think we all can admit that food

brings us pleasure which also means it's

good for the heart. That's why it's

important that you try and do small things

that can positively affect your health and

satisfy you as a person. This is why I tell

people to eat more fish: because there are

so many delicious ways to eat it and it can

be healthy for your body at the same time.

You can treat yourself to a snack that you love every once in a while, as long as you remember that it shouldn't be a part of your regular diet.

Mental food- Life with no balance, is a hangover- LOL

Eat balanced meals

If you have ever played any sport in your life, you understand that the most successful person in the game is usually the most balanced player-meaning that the most successful person is not the one who can shoot the best, or dribble the best, but the one that can do everything. The same goes for eating. You want to incorporate all five food groups into your diet. Try not to just eat meat and potatoes; mix it up! Okay, you can keep the lean piece of fillet but substitute some rice on your plate, and

veggies. Instead of A-1 sauce, see if they

offer any other alternatives- for example, a

blue cheese cream sauce which would also

help you out with your dairy for the day.

Just try and eat from all the food groups,

not just the same two. To let you in on a

little secret... it's not that hard to do.

Mental food- the only true disability is a bad

attitude- unknown

Make changes that you will be able to stay with over time

When you're trying to change your eating habits, there is one thing that you want to keep in your mind-and that's the future. You want to make changes that you feel you will be able to keep doing. That's why most diets don't work: when dieting, you don't really see yourself eating in a strict (unhappy) way for the rest of your life. The majority of people are thinking they can lose weight fast (whatever the reason) and

then they can just start back up with the old

habits and keep the weight off. That's why

it's important to take things slow.

Mental food- It takes old habits a little time to

die off

You need physical activity to support your

healthy eating

This may be the only time you will ever

hear me say these words in a sentence:

"there really is no point in eating healthy"-

if you're not exercising. Exercise also helps

to speed up your metabolism, which is a big

plus. You know how people always use

metaphors to explain things and it makes

things make sense? Well, it's no different

here. Eating healthy and exercising go together great like spaghetti and meatballs, or peanut butter and jelly, or how about this- scallops and bacon (that's for all the chefs out there- Lol). I'm no personal trainer, but I do workout regularly which means there came a day when I told myself it's time to get in better shape. It wasn't easy in the beginning, but now I can't go without it. The one thing I have learned through the process of getting from where I was to where I am now is that, "Discipline builds desire." Meaning sometimes in the beginning you have to make yourself do what you don't naturally want to, and eventually it will be your desire.

Mental food- Everyone is self-made, but only the successful ones admit it- Les Brown

Calories = energy, so eat as much as your body will use

Calories are not bad; they give your body energy, but remember that whatever your body doesn't use; it will store or get rid of. That's why everybody is counting calories these days. You remember how back in the Stone Age days the slogan was "You only kill what you will eat?" Well not that much has changed except we're not killing; we're just eating. Only eat what you will use. That's why exercising and eating healthy go hand in hand because your body needs calories- just not too many. The average recommended calories intake is

2,000 a day but this can vary due to a

person's age, sex, and level of physical

activity.

Mental food- How could something so bad be

so good?!?!

Everyone's body is different

We all know that no two people are the

exact same just because you and another

person fit the same description does not

mean that you need to follow the same

diet. Genetics plays a small but vital part in

the makeup of every human being so each

individual will need to adjust their diet to fit

their needs. Look at me, for instance; I'm 6

foot 4 inches 170 pounds, and very active

with a high metabolism so I don't

necessarily have to watch what I eat as

closely as someone who has the same

physical attributes as me but who works at

a desk all day, goes straight home after

work, and hits the TV. You may think that

you and another person who is similar in

body weight, age, and level physical activity should be on the same diet, but don't forget about those variables that you may have forgotten like, if the other person is eating very few proteins, their diet may include more protein in it, but if you're already consuming enough protein you will be overloading yourself.

* Mental food- The best person to be like is self.

Limit your salt intake

With today's various styles of cooking it shouldn't be that hard to avoid salt. It's when we go out to restaurants that we need the will power to cut back on adding salt to our meals which can really start to hurt you when you don't already know how much salt was cooked into your meal before it arrived at the table. Too much salt on a daily basis will increase your chances of having high blood pressure. I know it doesn't sound that bad but I'm pretty sure that no one wants to be taking pills for the rest of his or her life, if it can be avoided. This is what people need to understand: your kidneys control the levels of sodium in your body. If you have too much salt and your kidneys can't get rid it, the sodium will build up in your blood. This will lead to high blood pressure. Salt is necessary for our bodies- but not too much of it. Fast food is one of the top places where we consume dietary sodium.

* Mental food- Salt was created to preserve, not to destroy

Whenever you do eat unhealthy food, eat smaller portions, and eat less often

While professionals like me realize that you can eat almost anything in moderation and still keep a healthy lifestyle; it's not just the moderation that's key in allowing you to eat your favorite foods- it's also your discipline. When you do eat those unhealthy foods that we all love; make sure that you're eating smaller portions, or trying substitutes. I truly believe that you should, for the most part, only treat yourself to those tempting foods on special occasions like birthdays, Valentine's Day, Thanksgiving, Christmas, etc. Make sure you work it off the next day!

* Mental food- Sometimes great things come in small packages.

The Omega 3 fatty acids (fish oil) are VERY IMPORTANT

I have dedicated a section of this book to explaining the Omega 3 fatty acids. Just in case you skipped over that section, make sure you read this: taking fish oil (Omega 3) is one of the healthiest things you can do for your body. Your body cannot produce these fatty acids but it needs them to function properly. WOW- did everybody just read that? I said properly, most of us have never had our bodies function properly. Omega 3 fatty acids have many positive effects on your mind, eyes, and heart. I don't know about you, but those three things are very important to me. Finish in Omega 3 section…

Mental food- Most people are afraid to be the best version of themselves.

Help your metabolism

The first thing that everyone must know is the metabolism's role in the body.

Metabolism is simply the process of breaking down fats, carbohydrates, and proteins into energy that the body needs to keep running. People with slower metabolisms tend to gain weight faster. Facts about metabolism:

 *Yes- you can help speed up your metabolism

* Once you hit 40, your metabolism will start to slow down.

* If you increase your body's need for energy you will speed up your metabolism

* You will increase your metabolism by eating food that requires extra energy to digest (food high in protein and fiber).

* Your body is burning calories from fat, protein, and carbs, but you don't get to choose which calories are burned first. The only thing you need to know is that your body burns fat when it needs energy.

* *Mental food- Dear self, help me, help you.*

Choose foods that improve your health and stay away from those that hurt it

Yes, certain food help you lose weight and fight off calories; one such example is cabbage. Cabbage is high in fiber and low in calories, but **what you need to know is that it uses more energy to digest the food than the cabbage itself contains**. Also, oranges are supposed to contain fat blasting compounds. I also want people to know that when they eat foods that are high in protein, they burn twice the number of

calories during digestion.

Mental food- fill two needs with one deed-

unknown

When you go out to eat, don't eat your

whole plate just because it's there

When you go out to eat, keep three

things in the back of your mind when

ordering your food and eating: YOU, YOU,

and YOU. Almost 100 percent of the time I

think it's safe to say that restaurants are not

worried about your diet when they create their recipes (I'm talking about quality restaurants, not chains), chain restaurants are a NO, NO). At the same time, I think it's safe to say that in American restaurants, the serving sizes are too large. Most of the time when you go out to eat, the kitchen will put more food on your plate than you can handle anyway but as diners we feel that we have to eat it all to get our money's worth. Since most restaurant food is not healthy in the first place, when you do go out, order a salad and an appetizer instead of a large meal. Or try and see if you can split your entire meal; that way two people can eat for the price of one. At the end of the day you have to care more about your health than anyone else will.

Mental food- They say there is no "I" in team, but there is in victory.

Drinking just one 12- ounce can of soda daily can increase your weight by 16 pounds over time

If that fact doesn't open your eyes, then I don't know what will. I thought that it was important to share that because sometimes people don't realize that not all weight gained comes from food. Soft drinks also contribute to weight gain so when you change your eating habits make sure you don't over-look the types of beverages you are consuming.

Mental food- it's the small things in life that give you the biggest problem.

Our bodies are 75 percent water; drinking water will help aid you and or help you to maintain a healthy life

Each and every cell in your body needs water to perform its essential functions. Not only does water keep you hydrated, but it also helps to flush your system (kidneys and bladder) of waste products and toxins.

* Mental food- We never know the worth of water til the well is dry- Thomas Fuller

Focus on one food habit at a time

This is one of those topics that should have a star next to it because it shouldn't be missed. When people realize that they need to improve their eating habits, they usually try and change everything at once. This mindset will likely make you end up cheating on your new goals. Try focusing on one thing at a time; for instance, if you're just starting off, you might want to start with your beverages. Maybe you consume too many soft drinks throughout the day so you may want to substitute water and Gatorade for the first couple weeks until you adjust to the switch then move on to your next hurdle. Maybe it's including more veggies in your diet, whether a salad with your lunch or celery with your wings.

You must start somewhere, but you don't have to start with everything. If you're making the switch from less healthy food to more nutritious foods, try to make the change as pleasurable as possible- that way you stick with it.

* Mental food- Before you can tame the lion, you must 1st learn to tame yourself.

Try drinking a glass of water 1st whenever you are hungry

Do you remember when you were a kid and your parents would tell you not to drink your entire beverage before you ate because you would waste your food? There is some truth to that: liquid acts as water weight and helps you to get fuller faster. So now it's time to disobey our parents for the right reasons; so, from here on out you should try and drink a glass of water before

your meal to prove your parents were right!

Mental food- One of the cheapest things could have the most expensive effect of your body.

Learn to eat until you're satisfied, not stuffed

Yes, knowing when to stop eating has always been a problem for Americans; eating until your stomach can't take anymore is not the way to go. You want to be satisfied and alert when you are done eating not full and ready to take a nap-

although there are certain times when that

is suitable (holidays). Just remember how it

is when you feed a baby; seeing as how

none of us speak "baby" we usually feed

them until they stop sucking the bottle or

until the bottle is gone. What does a full

baby do next? Huh, I wonder- they usually

burp and go to sleep. It shouldn't be the

same way for an adult every night.

Distinguishing between satisfied and stuffed

is hard for most people because they are also eating too fast (do you see how each point ties together?). We never give our brains a chance to work with our bodies, so for that reason, we over eat and gain extra weight- which could be prevented by slowing down on dinner.

Mental food- There are two ways of being satisfied, one is to have all you want, the other is to be satisfied with what you have.

Missing meals is not a good way to lose weight

You want to eat in regular intervals, meaning breakfast, lunch, dinner, and snacks. Spacing food evenly throughout the day is vital to weight loss. You want to get your body in a routine for eating daily and getting the proper nutrients. It is a fact that people who skip meals are more likely to have weight problems because when they do eat, they're usually eating all the wrong things and therefore their bodies will be

lacking in certain nutrients.

*Mental food- Be calm and **orderly** in your life,*

that you may be violent and original in your work-

Clive Barker

Burning just a simple 50 calories a day equals five pounds a year

I wanted you to see that fact so that you might understand how even the little things can affect you in a major way.

You gain weight when...

you consume more calories than your body is burning and genetics play a small roll also about 5 percent (don't forget that). To be honest, I don't think I can put it any simpler than that; most people just need to adjust their daily activity and decrease the number of calories they eat. But don't get the wrong hint, because you DO NEED CALORIES.

Losing weight slow...

I am a big fan of people who choose to lose their weight slowly which is the correct way. Statistically, the most successful people who keep their weight off have lost it over a longer period of time. I don't like to do things more than once; I like to get the job done right the first time. That's why it's important to set yourself up for success, not just to succeed. What I mean by that is don't just lose the weight and think its over- yeeeeeaaah you won- because yes, you succeeded in losing the weight but now let's see if you're successful in keeping- it off, and the answer is usually no. If you know your will is weak when it comes to food; instead of trying to lose 20 pounds in two months, try to lose 20 pounds in 20 weeks. Doing that will give you the chance to lose a pound a week, which is super easy, and the option of eating more than you would on the other diet- that way, you have a tremendously smaller chance of quitting your diet. It also gives your body a chance to really adjust and get use to the new changes. Yes, it may take five months rather than two, but you're more likely to keep it off and still live a happy life.

Mental food- Remember the turtle beat the rabbit.

It takes time for your brain to make any change a repetitive behavior

Yes, there is an actual time frame for how long it takes before something becomes a habit: it takes 14 to 21 days of repetitive behavior to form a new pattern in the brain before something will become a habit. You need to keep in the back of your mind that yes, it will be hard- for instance, you may have trouble adjusting when you

start to eat the correct portion size but over

time you will do things without even

thinking about them. The key is to be fair to

yourself and give your new changes some

time before you kick new ways out the

door.

Mental food- There is more to life than

increasing its speed- Gandhi

You are supposed to drink eight glasses of water a day

It's crazy, but most of Americans live their lives dehydrated. At this point in my life, while I'm writing this book, I am also working as hard as I ever have; running a very busy restaurant "SuperChefs", doing a lot of public speaking, being a personal chef, on top of that raising my kids, and finding time to be a great husband. Since drinking water has been a problem for me, what I do to slowly transition myself to

drink the right amount of water is to make

sure that when I'm at my morning job, I

drink nothing but water. That way, when

I'm at my night job, I can have my sweet tea

or my no-good-for-you, Sprite.

Mental food- Drinking water is like taking a shower on the inside of your body- Myspawater.com

Eat a variety of different, colorful fruits and vegetables

When you eat a lot of different types of fruits and veggies, you're giving your body an abundance of vitamins and nutrients. It's also going to lower your risk of high blood pressure, help you control your weight, and lower you risk of heart disease. Veggies and fruits are great sources of Complex Carbohydrates which stabilize your blood sugar levels.

Mental food- Life expectancy would grow by leaps and bounds if green vegetables smelled like bacon- Doug Larson

Easy ways to get healthy food in your diet

*Add strawberry and bananas to your cereal

* Bring yogurt, a bag of carrots, or a cup of fruit to work with you every day

* Order salad instead of fries

* Dress your sandwiches with lettuce, tomato, or onion.

* Drink water whenever you're at home

* Put extra tomato and lettuce on that taco

Eat more fish and seafood and cut back on consuming meat

Yes, we all love a good rib eye steak, don't we? But that steak has a high percentage of fat while fish has the type of oil (Omega 3) we all need. I'm not going to stand anywhere as a chef and announce that people shouldn't eat meat because then I would be a hypocrite and misleading. What I'm saying is the proof is in the pudding (as the old timers would say):

people who consume less meat are living

longer and healthier lives. You can still get

your protein other ways. Don't take

anything I'm saying in the wrong way

because I eat meat just like a normal

person- except I do choose fish when it's

available (which is most of the time).

Mental food- I grew up my entire childhood

thinking that Cadillac was the best car, until a

drove a Corvette.

Avoid refined sugars

Refined sugar was once said to be one of the cheapest ways to kill the body (wow). They are rich in calories and are one of the primary causes of for obesity and diabetes. Refined sugars are any type of sugar that has been processed and examples include table sugar, sanding sugar, powder sugar, and corn syrup.

Over 60 percent of fruits and over 50 percent of vegetables are cheapest when bought fresh

There is no reason for anyone to still be buying canned veggies, unless you truly can't afford fresh. Please stay away from canned fruits, as they are always setting in syrup, which is packed with refined sugar. Making vegetable side dishes at home is simple, and many recipes can be learned easily online nowadays

Mental Food- You are what you eat, so don't be cheap, fast or fake- unknown

You shouldn't eat after 6:30 pm

As most people, can tell so far from reading this book, I am a realist; I know we don't live in this little make believe world as so many experts try and make it seem. Yes- you should eat dinner by 6:30 pm but come on- who wouldn't then want something later. Back to the same point I made in my other sections: make changes you can keep.

Try drinking water at night, or maybe even

fruit juice or smoothies. You don't want to

eat anything with a lot of calories because

you won't be active for hours and all those

calories will do is sit. This is also why

breakfast is so important in the morning. If

you eat late at night, you won't eat that

much for breakfast. Breakfast is the time

when you can eat the most. Also, your

kidneys are at their peak functions from five

to seven in the evening which is around the

time I eat my dinner.

Mental Food- there is a time and place for

everything under the sun.

Breakfast is the most important meal of

the day

Breakfast should get as much thought

as dinner does, if not more, because the

food you consume here could boost your

day or drag it. When you wake up, your

body is basically empty from at least seven

hours of rest so you want to make sure that

you start your day with some energy

because your blood level is low. A big

breakfast will help you concentrate better

and stay on your toes. Try to limit super

sweet breakfast foods, like doughnuts,

because they will raise your sugar levels and

you will be hungry shortly after. We all

know where that leads- weight gain. Also,

think about it like this: if you eat a big

breakfast, you have the whole day to start

burning those calories; where-as if you eat a

big dinner, you're usually going to sleep.

Mental Food- A bachelor's life is a fine

breakfast, a flat lunch, and a miserable dinner-

Francis Bacon

Stress also plays a factor in living healthy

Stress is a burden in everybody's lives,

but releasing it instead of letting it linger is

best. From all my research on and study of

stress, breathing was the one thing

common to combating stress. Breathing

deeply can help you relieve stress and can give you more energy. Just remember that living a healthier life has more to it than just eating because a person is more than just a physical body.

Mental Food- stressed spelled backwards is desserts- unknown

People of Longevity Rugao, China

When I first came across the gentle and kind folks of Rugao, I just couldn't stop researching them I just had to know how it was that they were able to live for so long. Then, once I found out as much as I could about them, I just knew that I had to share it with the world. The people of Rugao have over 250 centenarians, over 2,000 people who have reached the age of ninety, around 50,000 that are over eighty- and oh yeah, did I forget to mention that have they 5,800 people who are ninety- three? I just knew that whatever they were doing could help us out in some way shape or form. While researching, here are some of the things they do to keep healthy for so long....

* They eat very small amount of meat in their diet and they enjoy more fish.

* They don't eat produce that is out of season so they purchase food from the local market when the food is at its peak in

nutrition and taste. They eat a lot of

vegetables in the winter, like Bok Choy,

which is a good source of fiber.

* Most of their meals consist of rice,

especially breakfast; they are against having

a big breakfast because they believe an

empty stomach in the morning needs

lubrication before it is filled.

* The one thing that they do that was

unusual to see someone purposely do is

that they eat dinner during the kidneys

hours of peak- which is between five and

seven pm.

See- it's the little things that you can do

that will help your health in a big way.

*Mental Food- As long as you live keep learning

how to live- unknown*

Fish Oil (Omega 3-fatty acids): why

is it important?

In this section, I hope to show how

important the Omega 3 fatty acids are for

you and to encourage you to start to eat more seafood; nature's healthiest gift. Here are the facts:

* Fish oil is one of the best things we can give to our bodies.

* Your body needs Omega 3 fatty acids to function properly but can't produce them on its own.

* The fact is that you can't get enough Omega 3 from just eating fish because most of the world's fish have been contaminated

but introducing more fish into your diet is a great and healthy start.

* Fish oil helps to take care of your mind, heart, and eyes.

*How it helps your heart: fish oil is said to thin the blood which reduces your chance of a stroke or blood clot. It also reduces your triglyceride (forms of fat in the blood) levels and reduces blood pressure.

* How it helps your mind: fish oil also contains serotonin reuptake properties.

Serotonin is a chemical in the brain that helps to control your moods (Couldn't we all use that?). By increasing the reuptake in serotonin, fish oil can help fight depression and other mental conditions. DHA is another essential fatty acid found in Omega 3 that is known to improve brain function as well as improving communication between your brain and eyes.

* How it helps your eyes: fish oil helps to prevent macular degeneration, which is a

disease that afflicts one out of seven people; causing the central vision center to deteriorate over time. It will, in time, result in functional blindness. If you know anyone with blurry vision or difficulty in distinguishing colors and/or sensitivity to light, they might be suffering from it.

* Omega 3 is an antioxidant that can prevent damage by free radicals.

Things you should know

Yes, I know this isn't the most exciting subject ever, but I said the same thing in my CPR class, until I needed it- LOL. You can't do better until you know better, so that's why you see throughout this book that I give facts that may seem less interesting, but vital. I can't just give you what you want, I must make sure I'm giving you the knowledge you need as well. So please take your time and re-educate yourself on the facts most of us have forgotten about since grade school.

<u>What are carbohydrates</u>? Carbs provide the body with the fuel it needs for physical activity by breaking down into glucose, which is a type of sugar our cells use as a universal energy source. Diabetics and those with a family history of diabetes have to watch the number of carbs they intake because Carbs do break down into sugar.

<u>What is Fiber</u>? A plant based nutrient.

*Found in plants, nuts, whole grain bread, beans, fruits

* Helps you feel fuller faster and for longer (which can help prevent over eating)

* Helps to balance cholesterol

* A special type of carbohydrate

*Helps even out blood levels

What is Iron? Used to carry oxygen into the blood; oatmeal, black eyed peas, and chickpeas are all good sources of iron.

What is calcium? It is essential in the development and maintenance of healthy bones and teeth, and necessary for the function of muscles and nerves. Good sources include soy beans, collard greens, and turnips.

Foods that are low in cholesterol include:

* Lean red meats

* Skinless chicken

* Turkey

* Fish

Because those foods are also rich in protein, they will boost your metabolism.

* Breads, beans, potatoes, pastas, and cereals also help lower blood pressure.

* Fruits lower cholesterol because they are low in calories.

* *Mental Food- Knowledge, the cheapest thing in the world, but can make you the richest if you have it.*

Foods that help you, while you

help you

Cinnamon- can prevent an insulin spike

Berries- help you burn more fat while

working out

Almonds- can boost your metabolism

Mustard- can slow the growth of fat tissue

Oranges- contain chemicals that get rid of

fat, flavones

Soybeans- helps block the absorption of fat

Sweet potatoes- keeps insulin leveled

Asparagus- helps breakdown fat cells

Carrots- speeds up your metabolism

Cider VIN- apple cider vinegar contains

acetic acid, which helps speed up the

metabolism

I bet you didn't know

*It takes 3,500 calories to make one pound

of fat.

*Every gram of fat equals nine calories.

*More than half the world's population lives on a diet with the main staple being rice

* Fried chicken is the most popular meal ordered in American restaurants.

* Most of the nutrients in a potato reside just below the skin layer.

* Sweet potatoes and Yams are not the same.

* The most popular carrot at one point in time was the purple carrot.

* Believe it or not, lemons are ranked as one of the healthiest foods in the world.

* It's illegal to carry an ice cream cone in your back pocket in Kentucky.

* The twist in pretzels are meant to resemble arms being crossed in prayer.

* Apples float in water because they are 25% air.

* Apples belong to the Rose family. Yes, the same rose that you may buy for your significant other.

* Ketchup was used as medicine in the 1800s.

* Peanuts are not a nut, but a legume.

Throughout this book, I have given you my insight on many ways to positively affect your health. Now, the ball is in your court to use the knowledge that has been given to you. I am a big believer that whatever you want to do, or need to do, to get your

health to the place you have always imaged

takes a lot of sacrifice. You can either take

on hard decisions on your own while you

control the game or hard decisions will

come and wake you up and change your life

forever.

*Mental Food to go- Those who think they have

no time for healthy eating, will sooner or later

have to find time for illness- unknown*

Made in the USA
Las Vegas, NV
11 March 2022